Louring Skies

By William Radice

POETRY

Eight Sections   1974
Strivings   1980

TRANSLATIONS

The Stupid Tiger and Other Tales   1981
Rabindranath Tagore: Selected Poems   1985

William Radice

Louring Skies

POEMS 1977-1981

Anvil Press Poetry

Published in 1985
by Anvil Press Poetry Ltd
69 King George Street London SE10 8PX
and 51 Washington Street Dover NH 03820 USA

This book is published
with financial assistance from
The Arts Council of Great Britain

British Library Cataloguing in Publication Data

Radice, William
  Louring skies: poems 1977-1981.
  I. Title
  821'.914   PR6068.A24/

  ISBN 0-85646-153-9

Set in Ehrhardt
by Bryan Williamson, Swinton, Berwickshire
Printed in England
at the Arc & Throstle Press, Todmorden, Lancs

Contents

'Aeneas' was published in *Thames Poetry* II.10 (1982). 'People' 1 was published in the Arts Council's *New Poetry 4* (1978); 'People' 7 in *PN Review* 17 (1980); 'People' 1, 13, 17, 20 in *Babel* 4 (1985). Grateful acknowledgement is made to the editors; and to the Arts Council of Great Britain for its grant to me in 1980. The first of the 'Two Poems on Sad Occasions' was written in 1977 for the late Kanti Prosad Chaudhuri of Calcutta, and is dedicated to his memory.

W.R.

O sisters too,
How may we do
For to preserve this day
This poor youngling,
For whom we do sing,
By by, lully lullay?

COVENTRY CAROL

Two Poems on Sad Occasions

1

When the sunlight fades from the day
Or returns with the dawn anew,
Then who in the city can say
This matters to me or you?

We see through a camera's eyes;
We hear through the telephone;
So who at the sunset or sunrise
Can call its nature his own?

Only a birth or death
Restores the link in the chain:
At a first or final breath
We are one with the sunlight again.

We are chained for a breath and no more,
For joy and grief must be free
And the sunlight sets no store
By being or ceasing to be:

So we turn instead to our friends,
To the home and the telephone;
For our exile never ends
And all mankind is alone.

II

When the city sleeps at night
And quiet and dark is the sky,
We long to abandon the fight,
To close our eyes and die

And join the chain of peace
That links the near with the far;
Earth to earth's decease;
A streetlight to a star.

We toy with the half-belief
That peace in death is life,
Till we learn at the touch of grief
That living is tied to strife.

The familiar city street
Is null without noise and stress;
The darkened sky is the seat
Not of peace, but emptiness:

For the human friend that we knew
Lived just for this single space,
And the home of the mourners, too,
Is here, and no other place.

People

1 *A fourteen-year-old boy breaks off his piano*
practice to reflect on his new piano teacher:

My previous teacher said that mine
Were true musician's fingers, thin
And long; but his are short and thick,
Craggy, weathered, firm, like rock.
He says one's fingers must be strong
To make the piano dance and sing.
To make the piano shout and kill
One lets one's weight of body fall;
The greatest strength is used to form
Those softest dabs of sound that seem
To lift the heart beyond its beat,
Just as a dancer's feet are light
Whose calves are strong as piano-wire!
And this is why I'm still so far
From making the music match my heart.
He says that it will come out right,
My hands grow stronger, if I try;
But he must know that there's no way
These spindly fingers can be made
As strong as his, as firm and wide.
My previous teacher said that I
Was very good: one day I'd play
Superbly well. She made me vain.
She said my hands were long and fine.

2   *A woman of seventy lies in bed after the failure
of her first hip-replacement operation:*

Why does it all keep coming round,
The pain repeating in my mind?
The surgeon said I would be fine;
Thousands of people's lives had been
Transformed; surgery's major feat
Of recent years. I had no doubt;
The pain did make me wonder how
I'd ever move my leg, the day
They got me up to put my weight
On it; but surely they knew right,
I thought, and so I tried and tried
And managed, and was overjoyed.
But then it went, it was all spoiled,
Nurses confused, the doctor called.
'Don't fret,' he said, 'maybe you fought
Too hard. The joint has slipped a bit.
Lie still, and let me try and shift
It back.' And then that dreadful shaft
Of pain; and then the second start,
The second dislocation. Night,
New morning, one more fruitless try.
And now: 'We'll operate today
To get the muscles better trained.'
The nurses pass without a sound.

3   *A young man walks round and round his country garden
on a summer evening:*

I've never thought of this before:
To walk, not somewhere far away,
But here, within my garden gate,
Round and round, a steady beat,
Looking at things I must have seen
A thousand times, and yet not known.
This June has been so dull and cold,
But now the sky is clear and mild.
South-east is where the moon may rise,
And there it is, between the trees,
An edge of light, a growing gleam.
It seems to bode a better time,
A turning-point for me and mine.
I pass the apple tree again,
The disused well, the rebuilt shed.
The moon is where those trees divide,
And there it is, now half in sight,
Its beams beginning to transmute
My garden, boding something new,
A turn, a change, a better day
For me and mine. I pass the gate,
The broken wall, the mended seat,
The oak, and each time round I see
A bigger moon, and shining more.

4 *A forty-year-old spinster fears that her compulsions*
are getting out of hand:

I've heard of some who have to get
Stronger and stronger locks to fit
Their doors and windows with, and pins
And bolts and clamps and heavy chains.
At least I haven't reached that state.
The day's okay; it's just at night,
In bed, I get no peace of mind;
And what's so hard to understand,
I'm not in fact afraid some man
Will find a way of getting in;
So having stronger locks would give
Me no relief. I simply have
To check and check, both front and back,
I've fastened every bolt and lock.
I go to bed; it isn't long
Before I'm checking everything
Again, in case there's something missed;
But no, all done, all firm and fast.
To bed once more; and soon I start
To wonder if the back-door's shut;
And what is worse, I've now begun
To worry if some switch is on,
A light or fire; which means I'm not
Sleeping at all, I'm so upset.

5   *A wife of sixty-five mourns her husband's
latest infidelity:*

I loved you, but could not fulfil
All that you wished of me: for while
You had a careless, slightly wild
Bohemian streak, and loved the world
Of parties, I could never flirt,
Or dress seductively. My heart
Was more domestic, and my balm
Was reading, not some passing game.
I told myself: he needs to play,
To rove sometimes; I don't know how;
Let someone else. For I was sound
In my belief that, in the end,
Deep in your heart, you loved me best.
But now, after these years, that trust
Is frail: not that I fear you love
Another more, but that you give
Real love to nobody. You flit
Along life's surface, splash and float
And never look beneath. You go
Wherever it's warm, where you can lie
In sunny shallows, with your mind
Closed to the past or future; pained
That any should suggest you fail
Them; always sure they love you still.

6   *An old man, no longer able to look after*
      his back garden, laughs at his neighbours' concern:

I've heard their voices through the wall.
'Poor old man, how he must feel,
To see his garden gone to seed;
But these old people get so proud,
He won't let anyone come round
To clear it up. He doesn't mind,
He says, but I should damn well cry
To see my garden go that way,
To have to chuck the thing I'd made.'
They're wrong, they're wrong, it isn't pride.
Year after year, I gave my time
To make that garden bear and bloom,
And I'd have called a lazy fool
A man who, at the window-sill,
Could sit all day and get a kick
From seeing flower-beds go to rack,
The fruit unpicked, the lawn a mass
Of bindweed, thistles, rank goose-grass,
The shed, the rockery, fall apart:
For gardening was my great delight.
But greater still the joy that I
Now feel to let my labours go!
I did my bit, I reached my goal,
And now I've finished with it all.

7   *A young boy on a family holiday finds the walk*
     to a remote beach too long:

My father says we can't get lost;
We just keep north along the coast;
Why do you children walk so slow?
But now the sky has turned dark grey;
It isn't warm enough to bathe;
The wind is strong; the breakers seethe
Against those rocks so close beneath
This slippery, dangerous cliff-path.
Why do we have to come so far?
My father says we'll soon be there;
My mother says we're getting scared,
It's getting late, the weather's bad,
The wind is cold, the breakers crash,
The rocks are black and dragonish,
Why don't we give the beach a miss,
Go back for tea? But now he's cross,
And won't give in, and says we're soft,
And there's the beach, down to the left:
He's going to swim, and we had best
Wait at the top. The breakers burst,
Bashing the rocks; the weather's worse;
It's getting dark; I hate this place;
My father sees no need for haste;
We watch him swimming, small, wave-tossed.

8   *A dissatisfied painter decides that he must*
     learn his art all over again:

> So here's a way out of the wood.
> At last I've realized that I need
> To look more closely at its trees:
> For all who truly earn their praise
> Can keep not only sum and weight,
> But also separate trees, in sight.
> I tried to paint the wood entire
> Before I had the details clear,
> And so the wood is strange and weird,
> With no way out, for no paths lead
> From what cannot be clearly seen;
> And can the wood be clearly known
> Except by taking diligent note
> Of every tree, and getting right
> Their special shapes from every side?
> So here's a way out of the wood:
> Two years of pencil and sketchbook,
> Sketching the separate pores of bark,
> The veins of leaf, the bones of branch,
> The hidden roots, that inch by inch
> The total wood is taken in!
> And then to paint it whole again
> In all its colour, light and shade;
> But this time known, and understood.

9   *An unmarried girl of thirty takes pride*
     in the decoration of her flat:

> I'm single, but have not allowed
> Myself to slacken, and have made
> My flat my home. It's such a shame
> When single people slip, and seem
> To give up keeping their flats clean,
> And let the furnishings remain
> Just as they found them. How I've slaved
> At mine! You wouldn't have believed
> An old Victorian flat could be
> Transformed so; not that you could say
> It looked too bad, just that the taste
> Was so old-fashioned, for the last
> Tenant had stayed on here for half
> Her life. I stripped the paper off,
> Re-papered, made the floorboards strong,
> Re-tiled the bathroom, painted, hung
> My pictures, put new bookshelves up
> And got the kitchen into shape.
> And now it's mine, my own clean place,
> My style of furniture, my choice
> Of bright plain modern colours, foiled
> By patterned curtains. Yes, I've whiled
> Away whole evenings, starry-eyed
> At what I've done, I feel so proud.

10   *A part-time Justice of the Peace is smitten*
     with doubts about his work:

These thoughts I have make me afraid:
I feel that what is being tried
Is not this muttering, shabby line
But forces that you can't pin down
To individuals: football crowds
Send themselves mad; surely the seeds
Of this man's crime were sown by grief;
This girl has had no family life;
This woman must be sick in mind;
This boy found nothing to be gained
From honesty. Gone is the day
When you could happily ignore
These factors: moral life has borne
Such blows from scientific men,
Such mounting evidence of less
Free will; as though an iron vice
Were squeezing, flattening wrong and right,
Victim and rogue, to single state.
These thoughts I have make me afraid:
There seems no limit to their slide:
Murderers, thugs, in each you find
A clutch of pressures that defend
Their acts: till all say 'we were led'
Or 'we can't help the way we're made.'

11   *An attractive undergraduate compares herself*
    to the girl in the next room:

> She never lets up; she confines
> Herself to libraries; she moans
> If noise of friends or music goes
> On after twelve; she always wears
> The same old home-made skirt; her hair
> Is filthy. People used to try
> To get her out: one awful time,
> Punting, it nearly made me scream
> When all she did was lie and read;
> And when we stopped to eat she said
> She'd mind the boat while we all went
> Boozing. She can't bear pubs; she won't
> Dance; but it isn't that she's so
> Bad-looking; if she wanted to,
> With clothes and make-up she could soon
> Make herself nice, bring in the men.
> Of course she'll get a First: she says
> Never will so much time be hers
> Again, to read and think and learn.
> She wants to use it while she can.
> Neither shall I get this time back.
> Maybe she's right: she's strong, I'm weak.
> Who knows exactly what it means
> To make your hay while the sun shines?

12 *A young man discloses the secrets of his wardrobe:*

I go for sober public dress;
I hate to feel I'm out of place;
I favour suits in browns or greys,
With coloured shirts, but simple ties.
At home my guests will scarcely find
My taste in casual clothes profound:
Even alone, I sit about
In slippers, sweaters, and at night
I wear pyjamas, corded, striped.
But in my mind I've always kept
A store of more unusual dress,
And by my 'wardrobe' I mean this.
I've come to feel that it exists
As truly as its name suggests:
Even before I'm out of bed
I'm often daringly arrayed;
Or passing time on bus or train
I try my hats on, one by one.
Just now I wore a cummerbund –
The sunset was so wild and grand
I had to walk in clothes to match.
At night I sleep without a stitch.
My wardrobe closed, I lie in bliss,
Dressed in flamboyant nakedness!

13   *A young widow sustains herself by faith*
     in her husband's return:

I do not grieve, I do not yearn;
I keep my mind cool and serene,
Trusting in things that cannot be.
I have a faith that one mad day
I'll hear the car, the door, the same
Glad breezy shout, and he'll be home.
And so I tell myself: 'Suppose
He suddenly arrives, and sees
The mess this kitchen's in, the grease,
The washing-up'; and then I race
To put it right; or 'How ashamed
I'd be like this: my hair uncombed,
No make-up, clothes so creased and old';
And then I change. I've never failed
For long: the faith that has sustained
Me keeps my skin and body toned.
I tell myself: 'Even suppose
He comes on one of my off-days –
My face, my legs, my breasts will say,
"I have preserved myself for you."'
These notions are not based on truth,
But I can't live without my faith.
I do not cry, I feel no strain.
I live by faith in his return.

14   *A perpetual traveller prepares for another of his*
      periodic visits home to see his mother:

For each return and each goodbye
I have an image stored away,
Safe in my mind. She seems to age
– After the brief, restoring surge
Of welcome – more with my return
Than in the lonely years between.
I now well know that she will seem,
At first, no older than last time;
But when the brief, rejoicing light
Has left her eyes, a sudden weight
Of years will bow her body, drain
Her vigour, weaken skin and bone.
It seems that I'm the one who shows
My years at once: she always says
I've changed, matured; but in the end,
Leaving, I feel she has returned
To seeing me in my childhood world,
As though she thinks I'm not yet old
Enough to pack my case, to know
Which clothes to wear. 'Please stay, please stay'
Is in her eyes; but she's too brave
Ever to feel I shouldn't leave.
A stronger force has taken me
Away. She never questions why.

15   *A middle-aged clergyman struggles to pick up*
the remnants of his religious belief:

Now as before, I find a link:
Nature and Church have always sunk
Together: when the Church is dust
The Natural world has also lost
All joy, all wonder. Peace has gone,
The car says, and the aeroplane;
Purity, too, the tin cans say
To the woods, the filth to the sea.
However much I praise and kneel
The Natural sacrament will fail
At times of darkness, when my faith
Has lost its living heart and breath.
Beauty has gone, the tractor says
To fields, the suburb to the rose.
But in the past my faith has grown
Again, from whispers that remain:
A hovering, a call as faint
As song remembered; then by dint
Of work and thought the edifice
Re-forms, Nature returns to grace.
This time I fear that I may break
Before my joy and faith come back.
Nature and Church have turned so dank,
The call so faint, here on the brink.

16 *An amateur pilot revels in the freedom
and ecstasy of flight:*

Men who have seen the earth from space
Have known the same delight as this,
But vaster and more thrilling still:
For whereas from my cockpit all
I see is England newly born –
The fields so miniature and green,
The roads and villages so neat,
With all their dirt and mess smoothed out
That bind our spirits to the ground –
They see the entire world refined,
Transformed into an orb of light,
Brilliant and young, and can forget
The wars, the failings without end
That keep our tired souls earthbound.
And which is real? The view from down
Below, disordered, or the clean
View from above? Who knows? Maybe
I seek illusion as I fly,
But this is real, this urge to climb,
And astronauts must know the same
Tremulous poise of heart and brain
As I feel in my frail machine,
And more than I, know the release
That makes our earth a different place.

17   *An elderly father looks out of his bedroom window*
     at his schizophrenic son:

Often I try to trace the sad
Steps that so secretly have led
To the boy pacing, turning there:
And stupid images recur:
The smashed guitar he failed to learn;
The painted clothes, discarded, torn,
The mantra on his bedroom wall:
So secretly, because we still
Believed that such peculiar fits
And starts are found today in lots
Of boys and girls; but we were wrong,
Trying to understand the young,
Old parents as we were; and now,
Watching him pacing to and fro
Beneath the apple trees, suppose
One of the apples on the trees
Ripened from bud to flower to green
To red; but we let it remain
Alone, unpicked: the apple ails
And rots, poor boy, and then it falls,
And buzzing doctors chew the core.
Such stupid thoughts! I stare and stare
As if it's I who grips my head,
Wandering in the orchard, mad.

18 *An aunt of fifty takes pleasure in her ability*
to give imaginative presents:

I think that one can truly live
Only through giving: always I've
Tried to take trouble over mine.
I don't think I am ever known
To miss a birthday, young or old.
I keep the family carefully filed
To make sure each important time,
Happy or sad, returns to them
Each year. Some say a death is best
Forgotten; but not all is lost:
Flowers can show us what lives on.
And marriage can begin again,
Each year, with presents that I send.
Christmas I love; each year I find
I'm planning earlier: the right
Gift may be something modest that
I see in January: if you catch
The bargains then you don't spend much.
I always aim to spend enough
But no more; I'm not poor, but Life
Has taught me that the truly nice
Presents are simple, small, a piece
Of your own self. I do believe
The more you spend the less you give.

19   *A jaded woman of sixty carefully guards her inner life:*

Spent as I am, worn down by chores,
Cross with my husband, little stays
Of what once galvanized my brain;
But certain 'thoughts' are still my own:
Though housework long since killed my hope
That I would write, yet still I keep
My taste for what is good and real
In literature; and though I fail
To feel much love of life these days
I have a world of prayer that flies
My spirit to exalted heights
Sometimes; and thirdly, though the fates
Have ordered that I be betrayed
By husbands, yet a kind and good
Ghost that I know will still have room
For me when death takes me to him –
Dear ghost! How tenderly you sit
Beside me through the gloomy night!
And lastly, when I close my eyes
Sometimes, there are strange patterned ways
In which my thoughts are all explained.
My husband wouldn't comprehend.
I keep them safe: my taste, my prayers,
My ghost, my grasp of hidden laws.

20   *A young woman has mixed feelings about the patchwork*
quilt she has just completed:

Strange how two colours that combine
So neatly when compared alone
Can clash, now that the thing is whole.
I thought that I had planned it all:
I looked at books, gave careful thought
To getting every colour right,
Never afraid to change my mind,
Unpicking rows from end to end
At times; giving my very best;
Aiming at something that would last.
But now I feel this red's too hard;
I should have put that green outside;
The more I look, the less I like
The pattern of the central block.
Of course it's not completely wrong.
It's almost like a living thing,
A plant or child, that won't give in,
Entirely, to a perfect plan.
It moves along its own strange track.
Perhaps it's through a kind of luck,
Rather than all this thought and fuss,
That sometimes one achieves success.
All I can do is start again.
I think I know my next design.

Aeneas

AFTER AENEID VI, LINES 264-898

God, not of light, not omni-pervasive,
But source of all that is but is nothing –
Silence, emptiness; God of the shadows,
Help me to speak of things that are nowhere.

The smooth linoleum cushioned their footsteps.
Fluorescent lighting glared as if weary.
Notices showed the route at each junction.
Flexible fire-doors swished as they pushed them –
They reached the centre: strange-looking people,
Decrepit, dishevelled, pressed in around them –
Unshaven men; old women with make-up.
They saw a shop with sweets and tobacco,
Pens, cheap jewellery, cards and cosmetics.
People queued quietly, holding their money.
They passed still stranger people in wheelchairs –
Tangled limbs, gummed eyes, imbecile features;
Skewed mouths dribbling on chewed cigarette ends.
Their palsied lunging frightened Aeneas:
He shrank away – until his companion
Assured him all these people were harmless.
  They took the northern corridor: nurses
And porters glided past them like fishes.
The guide acknowledged each of them briskly.
She walked almost too fast for Aeneas.
They reached a door: the ward for admissions –
Pot-plants, armchairs, a long patterned carpet –
Sprang brightly upon them. Here the consultant
Sits in his office, fiddling with letters
And files, shifting from buttock to buttock,
Rubbing his beard. Too fat and unhealthy

He feels, too shabby, sour and hung-over.
His glasses slip; his jacket constricts him.
The long, light ward was dotted with patients:
A few hung round the door of the office,
Pestering nurses, hoping the doctor
Would pick them first. He stares at them glumly,
Then tells a nurse to call them in order.

  Aeneas watched the scene in bemusement
And asked, 'Nurse, why are some of these people
So young? And why are some in pyjamas,
Others in clothes? And why are they waiting?'
'These', said the guide, 'are recent admissions,
Acutely ill; such illness can strike us
At any age. Some are kept in pyjamas
Until the doctor feels he can trust them
Not to run away. The doctor will see them
In the right order when he is ready.'
Aeneas gazed and felt that these faces,
Though dazed and mute, were not as abnormal
As those seen earlier; almost familiar
They seemed, like silent faces in tube-trains.

  But now, turning, he saw, in the corner,
A looming form whose line he had surely
Known; and as this figure – white-coated,
A male nurse – neared him, shock and a spasm
Of fear shot through Aeneas; for here was
The face, the height of dear Palinurus,
Friend and companion, college coeval.
Taller than ever he seemed, and his fingers
Longer; white-coat and trousers ill-fitting.
He passed, arms crossed; he wouldn't have noticed
His friend had not the call come intensely,
'Palinurus! What on earth are you doing
Here? Don't you know me! Stop, it's Aeneas.'
He looked round sharply, embarrassed; but shaking
Hands quite firmly said, 'Didn't they tell you?
I left the college; this is my job now.'

  They sat. The guide had entered the office.
Palinurus told Aeneas his story,

Not quite at ease at first, but relaxing
Soon at having a friend to confide in.
'It is so hard', he said, 'to describe it
Except through images, and, overriding,
There is no image – nothing but darkness.
But often it's as though I am swimming
Against the heavy flow of a river;
No light; the flow is sullen and silky
As if a weir lurks too close behind me.
I fight for strength to master the current
But only manage not to slip backwards
Perhaps. Or else I'm lost in an ocean –
No flow; no wind – the weight of a leaden
Sick swell: I fight to keep myself floating.
Or else it's sand: I'm climbing a massive
Dark dune: each footstep slips, and the effort
To keep my ground is almost beyond me.
I feel great pain.' Aeneas observed him
And found no sign of pain in his features.
He seemed serene now: eyes and a tranquil
Half-smile strangely at odds with his story.
    'One thing has helped me through', he continued.
'In every age some people, I'm certain,
Carry alone the pains of the zeitgeist
– Or joys, maybe, sometimes; but the present
Time is unhappy, dark; an uncertain
Time, with the threat of utter destruction
From war or poison or over-expansion.
Such strains! It is my honour to bear them,
And the fact I'm surviving, despite all,
Gives me hope that the world will continue.'
He stopped. The guide was back, and impatient
Words came, 'Nurse, those beds are not made yet.
You can't sit here all day.' Palinurus
Stood up at once; the calmness fell from him.
Awkwardly shaking hands with Aeneas
He said, 'Remember, tell all the others,
Please, that I'm well and have not abandoned
My books; I shall return when I'm better.'

They watched him go to where, in the distance,
His lanky form could just be seen stooping
Over the beds, like a great white flamingo.
Remorse and grief took hold of Aeneas:
Remorse at having neglected a friendship;
Grief that his friend should be so deluded.
He stood, brooding, until the guide roused him.
'I'm sorry you were caught by that fellow',
She said. 'He should be one of the patients,
Not a nurse. Leave him. Come, we must go now.'
   The way seemed long: Aeneas was flagging.
He noticed that the floor sloped a little.
The air was stale, too – windows unopened,
With sickening smells of kitchen or Path. Lab.
They took a lesser corridor, empty
Except for footsteps padding behind them.
They reached some stairs, and saw the consultant
Nearly abreast; the hurry to catch them
Had made him sweat; his breathing was heavy.
They climbed the stairs together; the doctor,
More than once, it appeared, would have spoken
If cold looks from the guide had not crushed him.
They reached the second floor and he passed them
To climb higher; his wheezing resounded.
   The guide unlocked a door and they entered
The back ward. Here the permanent cases
Are kept: worn, inaccessible people,
Wrenched through the day from dressing to bed-time.
They suffer constant noise: of the wailing
Of some, of bathroom clangs, television,
Of who knows what weird voices inside them.
They breathe foul air; their clothes come unbuttoned.
Aeneas followed the guide. In the middle
Of the ward an old man was attempting
To bar their way with gestures and toothless
Sounds from his beard. A gift of tobacco
From the guide soothed him. Nurses were wheeling
Coffee and biscuits round to the patients:
Aeneas watched their looks as they guzzled;

He tried to see not bodies but people.
The way the nurses teased them depressed him.
He asked to go; they left by a back way.
   The mid-June mid-day sunlight was blinding
As the two crossed a yard and ascended
Shallow steps to the grass of the spacious
Grounds. But the trees surrounding the cricket
Pitch were shady and cool; it was lovely
To breathe fresh air; Aeneas had almost
Forgotten it was summer. They rested
Awhile on a seat, watching the distant
Revolving spray that languidly watered
The turf. It seemed alive: a reposing
Animal's flicking tail. All around them
Plane trees and chestnuts mingled their branches,
Drooping in the still heat as if heavy
With their own leaves. The grounds were a solace;
And though Aeneas felt that the sombre
Building behind them saddened their beauty,
He thanked God that such peace should exist here.
   They crossed the field and came to a still more
Secluded area. Smooth naked tree-trunks
Soared like enormous statues of women;
Intricate foliage splintered the sunlight.
They reached the edge and saw through the railings
That the woods went on, denser than ever.
Aeneas absorbed their calm melancholy.
Suddenly, near, he noticed two people.
They held hands as they wandered: the woman
Limped and tottered; the man was bent-shouldered.
They walked with heads raised, staring at nothing.
He asked the guide to tell him about them.
'Those two', she said, 'are always together.
They seldom seem to talk to each other.
Sometimes they kiss; he calls her his girl-friend.
There are more like them. Look, there's a couple
Through there.' Aeneas peered through a network
Of twigs and leaves, sun-mottled, and saw them.
He gasped. Although the woman was facing

Away from him, and leaves and her lover's
Bulk half hid her, he couldn't mistake her.
Wild, unaware of what he was doing,
Clutching branches, he shouted out, 'Dido,
Dido, no, no, it can't be – not you here!'
   He stumbled forward, crashing through bushes
To reach her. She turned slowly, and showing
No surprise fixed her gaze. He was speechless
When he saw how her features had altered.
The horror froze him: her handsome bone-structure
Puffy; her fine skin rough and discoloured;
Her hair in rat's tails; eyes that had loved him
Now bloodshot, fat, glazed over with hatred.
Sunlight framed her: a split-second image
Flashed through Aeneas's mind like a photo –
The round moon when it fully eclipses
The sun to become bloated, not subtle,
Not light, but dark and dully fire-haloed.
   With sinking heart he realized the rumours
About her plight were true, and he stammered,
'Dido, sweet love, I knew you had suffered
But I never – I fear that you blame me.'
'It's too late to feel sorry', she muttered,
And new misery scored through Aeneas:
Even her voice had thickened. 'You left me
Because you did not love me and selfish
Work and ambition always displaced me.'
'I had no choice,' Aeneas said fiercely,
'You know the force that urges me forward
Can't be held back: I tried not to hurt you
But you asked for so much; you would never –'
Tears welled in his throat: memories flooded
His mind of days when life had been happy –
Her soft arms and eyes; then the appalling
Strains that came from the struggle to please her
While fighting hard to meet his vocation;
And now the pain and guilt aggravated
By her being ill, her dreadful appearance.
Ignoring the guide and Dido's companion

He seized her hand and said, 'Please forgive me.
It's all over now. Please let me help you.'
   Her face was close, too close for Aeneas
To see anything through tears and the sunshine
Except the sweat that beaded her cheekbones,
Glistening like dew. Her breath was polluted –
He wished he could restore by encircling
Her with his arms her beauty and sweetness!
The man behind her lurked in the shadows,
Still as a tree. The guide was forgotten.
Removing her hand, Dido said coldly:
'I don't believe in help. I imagined
The world was good, that people if treated
With love returned that love; but your cruelty
Destroyed my faith. I grieve for the future
Of man. All one can do is do better
Oneself, where able, hoping for nothing
From others. I have made myself better,
Battening down great illness and weakness,
And the fact I've succeeded, despite all,
Gives me some hope the world will do also.
This sun, these marvellous grounds, are a comfort.
My friend is kind; we mean to get married
Soon. I'm well now.' She turned to her lover.
Aeneas saw him, over her shoulder:
A huge buttonless overcoat sagged round
His paunch; his eyes were bovine; his trembling
Hands, black, broken-nailed, played with a fag-end.
He smiled remotely. Dido escorted
Him off through the woods, touching him gently.
Sunlight sprinkled their backs like confetti.
Aeneas wept aloud, till he noticed
The guide sitting nearby on a tree-stump.
She rose and said, 'I thought I had better
Not disturb you. She thinks she's recovered,
Poor thing. Let's go. There's more I must show you.'

         *   *   *

Far, far appeared the ward for the dying
Pointed out by the guide to Aeneas
Across the empty, shimmering sports-field.
For all that the grass bloomed, his inertia
Made him feel he was crossing a desert.
As he approached the bungaloid building
He forced his mind to notice the wheelchairs
Lined in the shade along the verandah.
He knew the dozing occupants varied,
But hardly heard the guide as she told him
About each case; so numbed were his feelings.
The last in the line sat like a boulder,
His gums the only part of him moving;
His broken nose and forehead were sculptured
From stone; and when incontinence trickled
Before their eyes and darkened his trousers
It seemed like water sprung from a mountain.
The guide spoke on: Aeneas, half-hearing,
Tried to imagine wars that did damage
Like this: he touched the wiry-haired forearm
And the man shot back, fighting and gasping.
    They reached the door and paused on the threshold.
The guide, sensing her charge was distracted,
Spoke curtly: 'We can either go this way
Through the sick ward; or else, if you're squeamish,
Go by this outside path. We shall have to
Hurry to catch your father by tea-time.'
Aeneas peered in; after the sunshine
The ward was blurred; he watched it grow clearer,
Then stepped forward with new resolution,
Ashamed to shirk death. For here they are cared for –
The paralysed, the sick and the senile
When the will fails and only the body
Stays to be washed and fed; disinfectant
Cannot disguise the odour of faeces
Or the warm stink of mince and potato
That lingers on for hours after lunch-time.
The patients do not eat out of hunger:
Their mouths, like sea-anemones, close on

The offered spoonful merely by reflex.
They eat too much: too stuffed for a motion,
Their stagnant bowels leak diarrhoea.
The doctor orders an enema: stocky,
Gruff, she works like a vet or a plumber,
And the nurses, too – jovially wiping
An anus, singing along with the pop-songs
On the radio while dressing a bedsore –
Are outwardly kind but inwardly callous,
Just as the ward itself, which is gaily
Painted and clean, smoothes over the harshness
Of death. Aeneas stared and was sickened
Not so much by the ward as his failure
To respond to it deeply. He questioned
The guide mechanically: why all that yelling
In the bathroom? And why does that patient
Chew his bedcover? What are those medicines?
Why is that man strapped into his wheelchair?
He scarcely heard the answers she gave him.
   But then he saw a bed that was curtained.
The shapes of nurses moving around it
Shadowed and bulged the curtains; suspicion
Of what was within fixed his attention
At last. He asked the guide for permission
To look; she withdrew, shrugging her shoulders.
Shyly Aeneas parted the curtains
And at once clapped his hand to his nostrils,
For the corpse oozed with gangrenous bedsores.
It lay face down; nurses with masks on
Bathed the whole blackened length of the body,
Dressing the worst wounds, plugging the rectum
With cotton wool. But time was disordered
As Aeneas watched: the nurses were speeded
And jerky like an old film, and when they
Turned the corpse it flipped round like a puppet,
Heavy though it was; yet, as if dreaming,
He felt his thoughts swell: weird intuitions
Crammed each second: the film as the nurses
Bandaged the corpse's jaw and urethra

Changed to a murky negative: visions
Of larger reversals swept through Aeneas –
Of light to dark, of pattern to chaos,
Of life to death. He seemed to be falling
Down, down an endless shaft with no foot-hold.
　　Fragments flashed of the pain Palinurus
Had mentioned, but before he could feel them
A greater horror staggered him: glancing
From the corpse to the nurses – observing,
As the film switched to colourful close-up,
The skin above their masks, whether negro,
Chinese or white, then back to the body,
Then his own skinny hands, then the nurses'
Brows again, then the body, and so on,
Aeneas found no difference between them.
There had been times of joy, when existence
Sang, stones lived, and miraculous order
Explained all things; but now the inversion
Claimed him – patterned no less, but indifferent
To hope or love: a vast mechanism
In which the corpse, the nurses, his own self
Were swirled without distinction. In anguish
Aeneas's soul spoke: *'O whoever*
You are and where: O God, not of Nature,
But God of shade and silence, who neither
Appears nor speaks nor answers, what further
Trials will come and how shall I bear them?'
Dimly he saw the corpse being wrapped up
And labelled; then he felt himself pushed through
The curtains, and the guide was beside him
Saying, 'You ought to wash after being
With that corpse. Go in here – but be quick now.'
Cold water on hands and face steadied Aeneas.
He walked quite calmly out of the sick ward.
　　And now, though the last leg of their journey
Was longer and more winding than ever –
Doors, corridors – Aeneas's footstep
Lightened, as if at last he was nearing
The exit of a maze, or freewheeling:

And indeed the floor sloped very slightly,
Helping them on towards their objective;
And even before they got there, the booming
Dance-music cheered Aeneas – the bustle
Of patients on their way to the party.
He heard the guide: 'Each week there's a party.
Look –' and suddenly all was before him:
A dance-hall packed with movement and colour.
'Here, join the line', he heard, and was somehow
Now in a great circle of dancers –
Left hand gripped by a lumbering charge-nurse,
Right hand clutching a withered old lady.
Round and round went the circle: it billowed,
Too, like a windswept washing-line, inwards
And out, in time to the deafening music,
Party-hats bobbing like luminous clothes-pegs.
The guide was sometimes lost in the mêlée,
Far on the opposite rim of the circle;
Sometimes her face was almost upon him.
Slowly Aeneas remembered his purpose.
The guide was close again and he shouted,
'Where's my father? You said we would find him
Here.' 'Wait until the dancing is over',
She said, and once more sank into distance.
'No no, now –' but they'd turned up the volume;
The nurses dragged the patients still faster.

   He wrenched himself away. As he stumbled
Out of the hall, he saw Palinurus
Coming along the corridor swiftly.
Wildly Aeneas called without greeting,
'I want to see Anchises – my father.
Do you know where he is?' Palinurus
Stopped and replied, 'I don't think I've seen him,
But try the work-room upstairs. I'll show you
The way.' His friendly manner was soothing.
Aeneas's nerves were stilled as he followed.

   The stairs shut out the party. Aeneas,
As he climbed, thought with dread of his father,
Of how after so long an estrangement

They would react on meeting each other.
The dark landing on which Palinurus
Groped for the door-knob raised his foreboding,
And once inside, Aeneas could scarcely
Make himself look around for Anchises.
The room was almost empty, and unlit
Except by light from north-facing windows.
Beyond the cluttered handicraft-tables
A dozen or so patients sat quietly
As though enjoying the space and the stillness.
Aeneas heard Palinurus behind him
Say softly, 'There's your father – I'll leave you.'
He slipped away. Aeneas, heart thumping,
Was left to face the patients unaided.

    Abruptly, even before he'd distinguished
His father, the shout pierced him, 'Aeneas,
You've come – I knew you'd never desert me!'
And then his father's arms were around him.
Embarrassed, Aeneas backed from his welcome.
'Dearest boy, let me look at you.' Double
Pleasure and gusto sent his voice winging
Across to Aeneas as though they were standing
Under some cliff or resonant archway –
'I knew you'd come one day. Was your journey
Hard? I've been very worried about you.'
'I've been all right', Aeneas half-whispered.
For a brief spasm his throat was resistant
To more words, and he stared at his father
Unable to match the warmth of his welcome,
Unable even to note his appearance –
Whether old age had changed him: for nothing
Showed but his radiant smile and his well-pressed
Suit, as though he had ceased to be human,
Had become ghostlike, ageless, or maybe
A lovely thing in Nature, a flower
To which there was no means of expressing
Thanks, and which seemed cut off by its beauty.
And the same bizarre metaphor stayed with
Aeneas as – in search of distraction,

Something to say – he looked past his father
At the small quiet group in the corner:
For with their smiles as broad as his father's
And suits as neatly pressed, and with evening
Starting to swathe the work-room in shadows,
They glowed like flowers in midsummer twilight.
    'Who are these men?' Aeneas spoke faintly,
And yet his voice seemed loud in the silence –
'And what are you all doing here, father?'
'We're all about to leave', said Anchises.
'We've met to say goodbye to each other.'
Aeneas was nearly crushed by the struggle
For words: 'You mean the hospital says you
Are well now? That's good. How have you done it?'
He felt his body freeze as Anchises
Embraced him again and said, 'I shall tell you.'
    At first the things his father was saying
Eluded him: words flowed indistinctly,
At one with the grey shapes of the work-room.
As though accustoming vision to darkness
Aeneas slowly made himself listen.
'These forces' – his voice was firm as a preacher's –
'Making, breaking; creative, destructive,
Govern the entire cosmos. The former
Is source of life and creation; of beauty
And skill and love. Its rules give us freedom.
The latter is that by which we are hidebound:
The rules of death, decay, dissolution.
When people feel their lives are determined,
They hand them over to powers of destruction.
Here I have learnt I am my own master,
And powers of joy and freedom possess me.
I'm well.' Aeneas felt his attention
Wander again. He noticed his father
Had led him gradually nearer the window:
Indeed they now looked out at the darkened
Grounds. 'The world', Anchises was saying
Now, 'is beset with terrible dangers
From violence, weapons, greed and pollution.

When I was ill myself I was certain
The world was dying. Because there were forces
Destroying me, the world was doomed also.
But I have cured myself, and my victory
Gives me faith that the world will recover.
I look at the night, seeing not darkness
But visions of hope: of Nature perfected.'
 He rambled on. Aeneas thereafter
Only heard fragments – fleeting and patchy
As the gleams caught from windows or headlights
By the vague, trembling leaves of the plane trees
Outside. He was held not by his father's
Visions but by the trees in the darkness,
Their gently shifting outlines and shadows.
They revealed a far presence, a distant
Faith that was his alone, not his father's:
To each a separate healing – Aeneas
Could hear at last the emptiness speaking –
To each a separate healing, a separate
Hope out of nothing. Then, in the darkness,
He lightly touched the hand of Anchises
And found he now could answer his welcome.
 Fluorescent lights came on, and the busy
Voice of the guide was heard in the background:
'So here you are. I'm going off duty
Soon. Hurry up please.' Quickly Aeneas
Said goodbye to Anchises and followed,
Taking a backward look at the patients.
They appeared exposed, suddenly – childlike
In the bright light; his father included.

Two ways lead from the hospital: one way
For those unchanged in feelings that brought them
There; the other for those who have wakened
From painful dreams – and such was Aeneas.

Songs of a Schoolmaster

nam castum esse decet pium poetam
ipsum, versiculos nihil necesse est...
CATULLUS XVI.5

TO MY COLLEAGUES

Here are the Songs of a Schoolmaster I told you all I'd write:
I bet you never thought I planned to write them out of spite;
For spite is what you're going to get, and farts and burps and shit,
More thunderous and smellier with each successive fit.
No one will escape the blast and least of all yours truly:
No bunch of boorish fourth-formers was ever so unruly
As this rude, raging cock-a-snooking demon in my biro.
But what *did* you expect, you dolts? D'you think me such a tyro
As ever to think a teaching job could be combined with Art?
It drains me! leaving nothing more creative than a fart.
Did you suppose I'd let myself descend to poetasting?
Lyrics to gratify some jackass editor by wasting
My gifts on 'shapely lines', a funny metaphor or two
To tart up agonized banalities – and 'How d'you do:
I've published in the TLS, I am a genuine poet' –
Oh if they served such stuff to me I'd tell them where to throw it.
No, if a teacher's job is such it drives out inspiration,
I'll write not poetry but verse, in anger and frustration.
And if you ask me how I call this thumping doggerel *Songs*,
I say it's no less so than what our adolescent throngs
Dance to in foetid discothèques; so help me, old fourteener,
To make my songs, like theirs, get louder, faster and obscener.
Think of a swelling mountain stream, once started, hard to stop,
Begotten not by snow but someone pissing from the top:
And from behind each rock that's in its path it gets fresh issue –
Great steaming loads, huge frothing tubfuls, wads of toilet-tissue.
If some of you already find these opening lines abhorrent,
Wait till you've been scooped up by the whole grand stinking torrent.
But if you're game to swim along, willing to be insulted,

Then by the end some benefit to all may have resulted.
Just as we need our daily crap, sometimes we need a purge
For what we have suppressed so long – each loutish, foulmouthed
    urge.
Fat-buttocked Californian dames are taught the primal scream:
I'll show them stiff-lipped Britishers can also let off steam.
My mountain sewer will swell until it hits a waterfall,
And then – but wait and see: and don't suppose that after all
I just intend to tease: we may feel better rid of it,
But smear it on your silly gobs, you'll find that shit is shit.
I mean to make my satire stick, make sure it pongs and squelches,
I'll mix no perfume with my farts, no kisses with my belches.
The thoughts I've had to hide from you are blurted out below:
O colleagues, stuffed-shirts all of you, take cover, here we go.

TRAVELLING TO WORK

Let's start with each day's overture, my railway-ride to school,
Spent preparing lessons while the Aberdonian fool
Employed as undertaker for the corpse of a Department,
I mean the Head of Classics, leans across the train compartment
With comments on the weather, politics or British Rail –
But he can wait: I want to put myself beyond the pale
By praising striking railway-men and cheering on the vandal,
For loving what is loathed by most can cause as great a scandal
As loathing what is loved. I love you, union activist,
For all the (thanks to your disruption) lessons that I've missed.
How grand it was last winter when unusual ice and snow
Made even worse the cock-up of a union go-slow!
Pompous Tory pundits may dispute the unions' right
To hit the public – let them ask a teacher with stage-fright.
It may be cold and wretched waiting for a cancelled train,
But better to wait all day than face that fifth-form mob again.
Each time a train is cut the children on the platform cheer:
It might surprise them if they knew I always growl 'Hear hear.'
They might be still more shocked to know – if they're the ones who
    scrawl
Lewd diagrams and slogans on each train compartment wall –

I *like* to be diverted by a spread of coarse graffiti,
The more obscene the better, yes, I like them when they're meaty:
So roll on, happy hooligan, you're people saying NO,
NO to the city, NO to the system, everything's got to GO.
But steady now, I think this fit is getting cross too quickly:
My plan was to begin my Songs by being merely prickly
And let the true explosions wait till several pages later –
So back to being rude about my daily fellow-traveller.
The fellow has a heart of gold, but God he's such a bore,
Often when I'm trying to do my work I want to *roar*
If suddenly I feel the breathing of his soft refined
Scots vowels in my earhole and I realize all he's whined
Is something stupid from *The Times*, some blimp or bishop's letter,
Or else he's made some comment like 'We seem to be doing better:
Five minutes late today instead of yesterday's *thairteen*' –
Until I met this man I thought that Tories got their mean
And ugly thoughts from prejudice, but he really *believes*
In what he says. He thinks that he's a Christian, but it grieves
Him not one whit to see each morning when we reach our station
That marvellous achievement of Great British education –
The 'independent' and the 'comprehensive school' divide:
One way our neat grey-suited boys, while on the other side
Depressed and sour West Indian youths look daggers as they go
To their grim school – my colleague wants to *keep* the status quo!
Enough, my stream has got sufficient now to make it run,
But nothing compared to all the filth I'll add before I've done.

AT ASSEMBLY

Hurry to Assembly now, you louts – there goes the bell:
No time to take the register, but perhaps that's just as well.
The form they lumped on me when I arrived as green as grass
Was the wildest in the school, and registration is a farce:
I can't begin to shut them up or keep them in their places,
But in my heart I like to see them kick over the traces –
Horses are what they seem, so thick and heavy of jowl and hoof:
Keep neighing and galumphing, boys, keep smashing, raise the roof!
When first we met a year ago, some were timid and small,

But now you're all great strapping lads, as rude as you are tall.
There's one of them that's daily more Neanderthal and coarser:
To give a true account of him you'd have to be a Chaucer.
He looks as though he's just emerged from some Medieval ditch –
Great jaw, great nose, coarse haystack hair, so wild that he can pitch
A desk across the room when he is, as he puts it, 'rucked',
So rude that when I caution him he tells me to 'get fucked.'
I always get on well with him because I think he senses
That given half a moment I'd commit the same offences.
So swear and smash away, my friend, and dip your lips in vomit –
But where's my stated plan? Again I find I've wandered from it –
I meant to build these Songs up slow, to large from teeny-weeny,
The mountain-stream my model, or crescendoes of Rossini
(But not so elegant, of course, I'm closer to punk rock),
But here in just my second fit my verse has run amok,
And what is more I find myself admiring not abusing,
Giving the old two fingers, true, but don't suppose I'm using
These songs as just a way of currying favour with the boys –
I want them all, as well as staff, to smell my rudest noise.
Rush onwards to Assembly then, come *on* or we'll be *late* –
This stream of struggling boys is my shit-stream in fullest spate:
They pour down from the classrooms to the Hall like gushing sewage,
Twentieth-century rubbish all, vomit and shit and spewage.
Suppose they all in one fell blast were, right here, taken short,
Dumping it on the stairs like cattle – there's a pretty thought.
At once the stairs would be a slippery, stinking road to Hell,
And there's my stream of filth for you – but isn't it *true* as well?
Isn't the world through greed, pollution, weaponry-production
A sliding, slipping, stinking, rotting pathway to destruction?
But no more wild digressions – I can hear the organ playing:
Soon we'll hear the silly chaplain's haughty fluty praying –
'Let us pray for all who starve in less successful nations,
And let us pray for those about to take examinations.'
Doesn't he see the Church he serves with every pious breath
Is part and parcel with the frame that's doing the world to death?
At least *this* congregation knows the Church is a disaster –
'Come, come, d'you call that singing?' shouts our handsome firm
    Headmaster:
'Hold up your books, let's shake the rafters in the final verse.'

The organ wheezes louder but the singing is still worse.
Isn't he tall and masculine, that's why he got the job –
He throws a cricket-ball much harder than insults I can lob.
He's learnt that he's respected if he holds his shoulders stiff –
Forget the nervous way he keeps adjusting his midriff.
His tones may be Augustan, but in fact he's soft as custard:
Sit on the stage with him, you'll see how shy he feels and flustered,
How frightened that five hundred boys suspect he's second-rate.
It's then my heart goes out to him and longs – but it's too late,
I'm writing a poem of contumely and now that I have started
I can't attempt to rid the air of wind that I have farted.
The Second Master's fairer game, his voice, height, hair as meagre,
His skin as pale, as other parts are big and red and eager,
Judging by the way he ogles every sixth-form girl –
But now I find my Song has knocked my head into a whirl,
I need a good night's sleep to get my venom up again:
I've so much on my chest, to lift it all becomes a strain.

THE DIFFERENT YEARS

That's better now, I feel revived, thank God for sleepful nights,
Made sweeter by enjoyment of my matrimonial rights.
It beats me why insomnia is rife, that people fill
Their guts with pills and potions when a natural sleeping-pill
(A fifth-former will tell you so) is readily to hand:
You don't require a partner, you can be a one-man-band.
At least I'm not so prim as not to know the proper way
To start the night, and now I'm up and ready for the day.
I've washed, I've shaved, I've cleared my bowels and now I'm bright
    and raring
To sing another Song, and give my mental guts an airing –
That is, if still you're so obtuse you can't predict my meaning,
There's shit inside my head that also needs a thorough cleaning.
So out it comes, and if you fear my heavy turds will swipe you
Then get out of the way – or not – but don't ask me to wipe you.
My target is an easy one today, I'll have no trouble
In keeping up my anger: now my blood begins to bubble,
I feel my long-choked voice already rising to a screech

When I survey the shit amongst the classes that I teach –
The tots, the twits, the oafs: but wait, although my plan's in tatters
(I meant to build up by degrees) and perhaps it scarcely matters
If stools are passed in trickles or in one enormous clout
So long as we can somehow get the stinking rubbish out,
I'll work up through the age-groups, from the pixies to the giants.
I curse the lot – sweet innocence, morose teenage defiance –
For taking my attention when my heart's in other things.
It's *your fault* that my talent throws up vomit when it sings.
The time that I would give to poems forming in my mind
Is swamped by never-ending dratted schoolwork of some kind,
Reading the silly books we teach, or marking half-baked scribble,
Talking, talking, talking – to what effect? Oh it's impossible
These days to make a go of teaching kids to read and write
When feckless parents let them watch the telly half the night.
They come to parents' evenings and complain with anxious looks,
'We're worried that he doesn't read – we give him lots of books.'
They'd look still more pathetic if I spoke straight out and said,
'I'd like to know how many books *you* have lately read.
Your child will spend as many hours warming his little arse
In front of television as he'll ever spend in class
Or reading or being read to or even in conversation:
You ask why he's illiterate – well, here's your explanation.'
Look at the shining faces of our first years – it amazes
Them all to hear about the *sentence*: *they* use broken phrases,
Curses, grunts and patter from the American pig-swill
They gawp at every single night – and this is what will kill
Our marvellous English language, kill its life, its truth, its vigour,
No dialectal richness left, in standard speech no rigour,
And pigs are what we'll all become, our trough the telly-screen,
Forever grunting, 'sort of kind of like you know I mean'.
But back to what it's like to teach the kids in the first year,
So ductile at eleven years they give me diarrhoea.
It's such a cinch to make the whole class rock with laughter, stun
Them with some trick or gimmick, make them feel they're having fun.
It's Friday afternoon: Sir, Sir, oh please let's play a game,
Twenty Questions – Certainly, my dears, it's all the same
To me if that will keep the little buggers quiet and happy:
I'm not a bad child-minder, I can even change a nappy –

A skill I might need here one day after having refused
Permission to the seventh child who asks to be excused!
On to the second year, the twelve-year-olds, they're scarcely better:
The boys get more and more cocksure, the girls get slightly wetter.
I haven't mentioned yet, the school is going through a strange
Shift to co-education: like a monstrous gender-change
Some parts have got their girlish bits while others are still male.
God only knows if the result will be a butch female,
Charging hell-for-leather round the football-field, breasts flying,
Or if our standard pupil will be sweet and always crying.
Just think if *thirty kids* at once burst into girlish tears,
Got *mad on horses, passionate* – give me the smirks and leers
Of all-male fourth-forms anyday, their smut, their spots, their
    strutting.
I love a classroom *vibrant* with their lust, their sex, their rutting!
I love? What am I saying? Not only am I ahead,
Leaving the ghastly third year out, but worse than that, instead
Of keeping up my filthy stream of piss and shit and bile,
I find myself recalling fourth-form wankers with a smile.
A curse for every year then, from the twelve-year-olds once more:
Perhaps you find your lessons fun; for me they're just a bore,
None more so than the crazy prancing round the junior hall
That's just young children's play but which we fashionably call
'Drama' – 'Come and watch us, Sir, we're ready', come their
    squeals –
I stand and vaguely watch the children rolling round my heels.
I'll leave them where I piss on them, or would if I were free
To do the things I feel; it's quite another cup of tea
With third-years, thirteen-year-old horrors, for it's they who piss
On me, the cruel little buggers – oh they never miss
A chance to score against me, it's the age they learn group-power:
They are (to keep my metaphor) a stinking sewage-shower.
I'm no authoritarian and they scare me to the quick –
Like dogs they nose this out at once, try every nasty trick.
All I can do is dish out exercises, make them write,
And pray it won't be noticed through the door I've lost the fight.
Teaching the fourth year, I've already said, is just a plunge
Into the cess-pool of their minds, you have to let its gunge
Cover your face as thick as theirs to keep the classroom quiet:

Try to haul them out of it, you'll get a bloody riot.
The fifth year's just a crazy race to get them through their O's,
Bashing away at punctuation, dragging them by the nose
Through Shakespeare: might as well be Japanese for all he means
To thick South London petit-bourgeois philistines in their teens!
And now the sixth form – bolshy lot: I feel so bloody tired
After those thirds and fifths, yet I'm supposed to sound inspired
About *King Lear*: for Christ's sake, every yawn, fidget and cough
Tells me that all you want to do is tell me to FUCK OFF.
Well, I'm exhausted, no strength left to give a fairer view
Of you than you appear to have of me, so SAME TO YOU.

LUNCH-BREAK

Colleagues, you may think so far you've got off rather lightly
And that my mood's in fact as jovial as my verse is sprightly,
But read on and you'll realize that it's nothing of the sort.
Maybe I've used more slang and ribald humour than I ought.
Today I'll write of lunches, and I hope that as I chew
Through chips and suet-pudding I shall get my teeth in you,
For lunch is the occasion when my anger really *burns* –
Your company disgusts me, while the vile food always churns
My stomach into raging storms of flatulence and acid.
To think you've never known this and consider me a placid,
Gentle, serious young man, an aesthete and a scholar!
Well, now I'm going to come clean, grab each one of you by the collar
And bellow down your earholes: 'I despise you, I do NOT
Adhere to your inane assumptions, I reject THE LOT.'
But first let me revive the image given at the beginning,
In case – assuming you're not prudish – it just left you grinning,
I mean my gushing stream composed of piss and excrement:
It stands for more, far more than just abuse and discontent –
There's pain in it and misery, others' as well as mine.
Picture its noble setting, the *élan* with which Alpine
Or Himalayan mountain ranges soar to a brilliant sky:
The snow appears so pure, the noble peaks seem to defy
All that man can do to make our nether world infernal:
At least this rock and sky and snow still honour the Eternal.

But that's not so, for nothing's safe and human sin besmirches
Even sublime mountains; hence my stream – it seethes and lurches
Down from poignant heights of sky, down from the gleaming snows,
Despoiling beauty, poisoning air and Nature as it goes –
The effluence of the twentieth century – oh my metaphor
Should now speak clearly to you if it's not been clear before:
For what is hunger in the world if not the foul excreta
Of nations where each person is a selfish over-eater?
And what, pray, is industrial dirt and world-wide devastation
Of forests, wild-life, if not massive greed and defecation?
And what are all those weapons set to hurl us to the pit
If not an ever-growing world-engulfing pile of *shit*?
I can't believe that when I sit attempting to hob-nob
Politely during lunchtime and my head begins to throb
And sweat comes and a dreadful, sinking sickness in my bowel,
It's just because the talk's so boring and the food so foul,
Nor because the hall is such a hell of noise and clatter,
Nor because I'm such a flop my harder lessons shatter
My nerves so badly they may one day drive me to a shrink –
No, these are not the reasons why I feel so near the brink.
Rather it seems that I'm a vessel for some larger terror,
A potty for the great earth-smashing turd of human error!
But cut the metaphysics, I've got more straightforward throws
And punches up my sleeve before my pain gets grandiose.
On then, on and on, and I'll begin with what we eat,
From soup that tastes like horse-piss to the technicolour sweet.
There's something in the way these stolid teachers nobly pile
Their plates with food so copious yet so greasy and so vile
That's *so bloody British*. Oh just as we held violent sway
Over half the world, and bled it, and described this as 'fair play',
And just as Ministers of Defence come out with criminal lies
That cloak the latest plans for sweet mass-murder in such guise
As 'To ensure security deterrence must be credible',
Likewise do we stuff our maws with bilge and think it edible!
Look at the way that silly fool, already overweight,
Takes chips, rice and spaghetti *mixed together* on his plate;
And look at how that other bugger doesn't seem to worry
When served a slop of vomit mixed with shit described as curry!
Maybe after forty years your stomach finds it easier

To get its faeces ready-made; thank God that I am queasier,
And thank God I'm not yet inured to being nauseated
By the gas with which my colleagues' conversation is inflated:
The endless talk of sport, the half-baked Tory politics,
The two together: 'Did you see that leftie *knocked for six*
In last night's *Panorama*? Russia's *scored another goal*;
It's time they *blew the whistle* on those scroungers on the dole;
The country's in an awful mess, we're *on a sticky wicket*;
Dreadful all these strikes in hospitals, *it isn't cricket*.'
Before the last election how they rattled just one sabre,
The same clichés from each; and when I said I'd voted Labour,
For all the boys might make a din and crockery might thunder
I sensed their icy silence at my sin and social blunder.
'This is an independent school, you can't *let down the side*'
Is what their stony stares suggested; yet I had to hide
My answer: 'True, and that's why I shall leave. I hope and pray
This year will be my last, but just in case I have to stay
I'll keep my nose clean. Meanwhile all the snot I sneeze or snort
I'll save inside my handkerchief, and when I can't be caught
I'll smear it over you' – which as you see I'm doing now;
And come to think of it, my snot's a weapon I've somehow
Not thought of till this point; it raises interesting ideas
(Although of course my arse remains chief fountain of my jeers).
There is another weapon, too, that my first song suggested –
I ought to dredge it out now, I'm so stuffed and indigested
From yet another meal of soya-mince and soggy chips –
So now before I end this song and wipe my greasy lips
Let us stand up, gentlemen, I have a solemn duty:
This BURP is aimed at you, and I shall make it long and fruity.
Be sure to breathe it deeply, for it's not just from school-food,
Nor have I simulated it in order to be rude,
No, it's made of flatus that *you* windbags all expel,
Breathed in by me, so what I breathe out is *your* rotten smell!
So *deep breath now*, and may I reach our fine lady Prime Minister:
To think that all you blockheads never seem to find her sinister!
One day when she's had her will and turned our crowded land
Into a nuclear graveyard, *one* day you will understand,
But only for a few minutes before you're burnt to death
(If you're among the lucky ones) – oh damn, I'm out of breath,

I've used up all my temper for today now and I find
This crazy song has not quite gone the way that I designed.
I wanted *vignettes* of the staff whose views I so despise,
But all I do is blast them all *en bloc* and generalize.
Tomorrow I've another vital theme lined up – oh hell,
I hope that I don't go and make a mess of that as well.

MYSELF

I wrote myself out yesterday, I've got an aching head,
But often it helps one's mood to get the wrong side out of bed,
Especially when one wants a mood that's black and full of spleen:
It may be bad for sonnets, but it's great for the obscene.
I'll let each ache and pain direct me, nightmares that I dreamt
Last night; for yes, today my subject is my self-contempt.
I'm starting with my body, so I want it to the fore,
I want it full of cricks and pains and wind I can't ignore.
Oh what possessed God to devise an evolutionary freak
Like me, or maybe I should say *like Man*; what fit of pique,
What wry sadistic joke by some insane cosmic creator
Produced this clever-clever puny violent fornicator?
And here you have in me a prime example of the breed,
As desperate in his lust as he's insatiable in greed,
But built in such a way that he's a failure every time,
Too odd to be Don Juan, yet too weak for violent crime.
He's like a walking Eiffel Tower with two supports not four:
A joint-fart from a third-form sends him thudding to the floor,
Or would if you would try, boys. Taunt me, ridicule my size,
My lengthy nose and fingers, and my manic bulbous eyes;
But nothing you could ever do could make me more aware
My body's ample cause for you to point and laugh and stare.
Perhaps you'd be surprised – that is, if you could extricate
Your tiny minds from telly, sport or 'why's my voice so late
To break, when Billy next to me is growing a moustache?' –
Perhaps you'd be surprised if you could know how crude and harsh
My thoughts are on the parts of me I usually don't reveal –
I don't just mean the 'private parts' my threadbare clothes conceal
(Although in that respect I'm quaint as any human being) –

I mean the parts that hurt. Oh why do people keep on seeing
A split between the body and that chimera called the Mind?
For clearly such a difference is impossible to find.
Curses on the rowdy kids that set my nerves a-quiver,
But fouler curses on that silly weakness in my liver
That all my life has tortured me with bouts of stomach-ache;
Curses on that Lower Sixth whose aggro makes me quake,
But viler curses on the sweat that freezes on my palm;
Curses on a profession which is never quiet or calm,
But filthier curses on a head and scalp that's never free
Of aching of some kind or other. Oh what agony
It is sometimes to turn the door-knob, face another form
When eyelids won't stop flickering and your head's a raging storm,
And what is worse, *the kids don't know*; a teacher has to *act*,
Not just in the way he holds a class, but in the fact
That like an actor he must make sure no one ever tells
He's suffering from another of his dreadful nervous spells.
Those who aren't like me can never know how idiotic
It feels to have the constitution of a prize neurotic.
Some people get the blues sometimes and call themselves depressed;
They don't know it's the *flesh* through which neuroses are expressed.
Ambiguous as libido, but in miserable reverse –
Body or mind? Who knows? We lust in mind but always curse
The *flesh* for being such a nuisance, kick against our pricks:
I'm trying to read *The Guardian*, why disturb me with your tricks,
You cocky little fellow? Oh dear, perhaps I should explain
I don't mean some third-former but another sort of pain;
For don't imagine that because I'm such a mental case
My mind's so full of tension that it hasn't any space
For lustful thoughts – far from it, and what might seem even stranger
To those who think they know me, I would be a public danger
If I were not so *self-controlled, mature, well-educated*;
My *super-ego* keeps me clean and outwardly-castrated.
These Songs are so outrageous I don't care if they incriminate
Me even more, so, wait for it, I'm utterly indiscriminate.
A fourth-former is speaking on 'The Future of the Race' –
I don't know what he's saying but I like his pretty face;
That sixth-form girl complains she finds *The Reeve's Tale* 'rather
crude' –

I pass the time in thinking what she'd look like in the nude;
Exuberant third-years keep on popping up and down like devils –
But if they took their clothes off I'd be Master of the Revels.
And that's not all, believe me, I am such a desperate fellow,
Many's the time, in Orchestra, my thoughts desert my cello,
Turn to my fellow-cellist with more ardour than they ought,
And long for her to be a mistress of another sort.
Suppose, my love, one day we played *one* cello, don't you know:
I could do the fingering and you could hold the bow!
The clothes you wear day in day out have got so soiled and crumpled,
It wouldn't matter if they got still further stained and rumpled.
Or better still, perhaps, the two of us could get undressed,
And I could rest my vertebrae upon your ample breast.
Even my male colleagues sometimes rouse my wicked blood,
The Head of English is such a dear I sometimes fear a flood
Of mad, obscene attraction, quite impossible to resist,
Resulting in that good man being passionately kissed –
Or worse. You know I get such thoughts sometimes, so wild, so lewd,
I feel as if the whole wide world were waiting to be screwed.
Just as a little baby seems to find the whole world suckable,
There're moments when I feel the entire universe is fuckable!
But God, what am I saying? You may think from the above
My Songs are running out of spite, becoming Songs of Love,
That all the shit and refuse in my stream will soon have sunk
Beneath a more torrential tide of universal spunk.
Fuck me if I haven't gone and let this crazy flow
(Nearly a hundred lines today in one almighty go)
Carry me hurtling onwards to some unintended region:
My thoughts seem as unruly as my thudding rhymes are legion.
Too bad, I've done enough, I'll have to end my song like this.
It's late, I'm starving hungry and I'm dying for a piss.

THE COMING WAR

I'm shocked that when today my theme's so frightening and so black
Last night my singing reached its end on such a merry tack.
But that's how nearly everybody carries on today –
We laugh, we love, when every minute death is minutes away.

Some people say, so what? In any case we're born to die.
Perhaps as far as I'm concerned there are three reasons why
I can't be such an ostrich. First, I'm vain enough to care
About my poems, whether, when I'm dead, they'll still be there
(It seems to be unfashionable to want one's poems to last)
To speak to fellow men just as the poets of *our* past
Can move us with their truth, their hope, their grief, their love, their
    joy.
Second, I am a teacher, and in every girl or boy,
In every face at every desk there is a clarion-call
To everyone to fight to make a future for them all.
And third, I have a baby daughter: when I watch the light
Dance in her eyes I want to cry, I want to shout, *what right*
Have men of power to threaten such as her with sudden death?
No cause is worthy if it costs a single baby's breath.
Perhaps now you're all wondering why on each preceding page
I've blurted out obscenities. I'll tell you: only Rage,
Rage at ourselves and what we've made will put the world to rights.
And if you think it's strange that I have levelled my bitter sights
On a good school, on schoolmasters who wouldn't hurt a fly
(Myself included), then I challenge each of you to try
To find ways to absolve yourself from all that men have done.
It won't be long before you accept that there are *none, none.*
Not for nothing do Roman Catholics talk of Original Sin:
I'm not really a Christian, but I'm sure we shan't begin
To save ourselves until we've climbed the cross of human wrong.
I want this, not foul streams, to be the emblem of this Song –
I mean the Crucifixion: it's a myth that still has force,
Applied to our own ever-failing suffering selves. Of course
I don't say we should start to think we're each a new Messiah –
I'm saying the strange old tale might still have power to inspire
Us all to *feel* the weight of human sin and grief and pain.
Only then will a change come, a chance to rise again.
Small hope. My Bible-knowledge being typically slim
I read it up this morning, and it seemed to me the grim
Elements of the story are the ones that are most telling:
The dark over all the land and Jesus Christ in agony yelling
Eli, Eli, lama sabachthani; the quaking earth,
The rending rock; suggesting the world's end, not its rebirth.

It shows us also what befalls a man who sees and warns –
Abuse and mockery, spitting, smiting, slander, the crown of thorns.
Isn't that, you may ask, what you have lapsed to in your writing?
I have two answers: first, it's human *folly* I'm indicting –
You'll find no genuine cruelty, nothing murderous or sadistic,
No violent act, no guns, no tanks, no bombs, no huge ballistic
Missiles; second – how quaint to find the sad old cliché true –
You may think I've abused you, but it's *hurt me more than you.*
It may be fun sometimes to let rip, 'let it all hang out',
Throw off one's inhibitions, let one's hair down, rage and shout
Obscenities at everyone; but when these Songs are finished
I know full well the fun and games I've had will be diminished
By having to hand them out to those who've liked my poems before:
I've no desire to make a scene or shock my mother-in-law.
Life would be easier if my poems stayed socially acceptable;
I can't deny my background, intellectual but respectable.
I know I shall outcast myself somewhat by these polemics
With family, in-laws, critics, teachers, poets, academics.
Obscenities! What irony some harmless little word
Describing a natural function can embarrass us if heard.
Aren't bogus words obscener, words by which we can forget
Our meaning? 'Missile' instead of bomb; 'deterrence' instead of
    threat;
'Theatre' for the region where the war might be contained,
i.e. the whole of Europe – perhaps they *would* be entertained,
The strategists and planners – perhaps they *would* enjoy the thrill
Of watching screens deep underground, assessing 'overkill',
Counting the 'megadeaths', the 'strikes', the cities 'taken out',
When my death, your death, his death, her death's what this war's
    about.
The Arms Race is obscene, its cost is hunger and inflation,
A thousand pounds a minute spent on arms when mass starvation
Murdered, last night, forty thousand children under three:
They died that we should die from megatons of TNT,
Or perhaps from something fancier – nerve gas, human pesticide,
The neutron bomb – 'cleankill' they call these things for they provide
A way of killing people leaving 'plant' and 'stock' intact.
It's all obscene, not just because it's foul, but in the fact
That like sex and excretion it's so furtive, secretive:

We're fools to think that ministers or 'spokesmen' ever give
The truth. In warfare, Churchill said, 'lying is indispensible';
So in preparing war, to lie is equally defensible.
The Government issues pamphlets which maintain the sick pretence
That Britain could 'survive' the war: they call this 'civil defence'.
We need cruise missiles 'in response' to Soviet 'advance';
It's they not we are always said to lead this crazy dance.
Britain is 'undeveloped' in the 'germ and chemical field';
D'you mean that forty years at Porton Down have had no yield?
What of the growing sale of our 'nerve-gas protection suits'?
The scientists who lend their skills to war are prostitutes.
It's all obscene and blasphemous. Sometimes I rub my eyes.
President Carter, 'Christian' that he is, can authorize
'The largest building project in the history of civilization' –
To glorify it? No, to hurry on its termination.
Two hundred rockets, ten heads each, each of three million tons
Of TNT; ten thousand silos; a crazy hide-and-seek.
Is this my world? Or does this article in the paper speak
Of some insane, baroque, Satanic, monstrous science fiction?
No, it's true, and likewise true our moral dereliction.
We're all responsible. I take the school at which I work
As fitting symbol of the way our world has gone berserk:
I mean the way we all fly off in disparate directions.
A school, just like society, falls into separate sections.
Ah Mr New Master, we need assistance in the corps –
No thanks, I'd rather not, I'm not much interested in war –
This is the room to which the children come to study history –
All those maps and dates and charts, you know, but they're a mystery
To me – You don't come up here much if you're a scientist –
You're usually in the lab, the others don't know we exist
Most of the time – The trouble is the boys do so much sport
Music hardly gets a look-in – I don't think they ought
To waste their lesson time on arguments on politics –
Art and Sport and Science and War and Politics don't mix –
I must admit to you that I'm politically naive –
Talk to the Chaplain, he's the one who knows what we believe –
Fragments, bits and pieces – I'm afraid it's not my line...
If we keep on abdicating, homo sapiens will resign
The earth one day to ash and dross and smoke and radiation.

I feel so weak and sick. I keep remembering a quotation
From Lord Mountbatten's Strasbourg speech, the last year of his life:
He, if anyone, knew the truth of weaponry and strife.
He said a nuclear war could *not* be 'limited in scope'.
All rockets would be fired: 'there'll be no help, there'll be no hope.'

FAILURE

I've missed a day, but far from feeling better for my rest
I feel like some long-distance-walker starting the day depressed
At having to lift his pack again, walk off his aches and pains,
Or like some weary husband whose intense profession drains
Him of the strength to prove his love by simulating lust –
No wish to copulate tonight, but conscience says he must.
It's true it was my plan to let my rage suddenly flag
After its climax; furthermore (the cat's out of the bag)
My scheme has always been to change my agony to love –
That's why I've hinted, here and there, I'm actually a dove,
No raging lion at all; but what I haven't said is that
(Although the Crucifixion maybe made you smell a rat)
The love would be no cosy thing, but large and passionate.
The rage, the thundering stream of shit would suddenly abate
After a waterfall, become a river pure and wide,
Rolling grandly on through pre-lapsarian countryside.
I'm purged all right today: I feel no wish now to insult:
But never did I think this weak, grey impotence would result.
The river may be pure now, but the land through which it flows
Seems to be just the land through which my train each morning goes –
The flat South London suburbs, under a damp, English sky;
The rows of small back gardens where some people like to try
To make a patch of Paradise with water, earth and seeds,
While others have no urge to clear the rubbish and the weeds.
Perhaps it serves me right: poems should not be propaganda:
My climax was a sermon, hence this present dull meander.
Perhaps as after sexual intercourse I'm simply sated:
Passion is never so sublime after it's consummated.
A climax is an anti-climax, true of nuclear war
As well as sex: 'So this is what man was created for –'

Will be the almost casual message of each mushroom cloud,
And irony, not tragedy, will be our murky shroud.
It isn't that I can't upon more temperate reflection
Think of ways in which I hold my colleagues in affection,
And pupils too: my love to every one of you, my friends.
I feared that when these Songs were done I'd have to make amends
For being so unkind: in fact I kept on stopping short
Of personal abuse: all I could do was shout and snort
In general terms. There was some nastiness when I began
The Songs, vented on one or two – but each so kind a man
That he will let it pass. Colleagues, I think that to describe
You now would be impertinent – more than my diatribe;
And pupils: the bright fourth form that would eat out of my hand;
The rowdy but endearing fifth, the loyal and generous band
Of sixth-formers who worked so hard, did well in their exam –
You know who you are, and I think you know the man I am.
I could describe the special days – excursions; wild, convivial
Ends of terms; the Calais trip – but it would be so trivial:
I wanted something bigger – yet that would be so untrue:
The cosmic love of those who, whether Christian or Hindu,
Bask in the certitude of some grand spiritual revelation.
It seems so selfish, fruitless, void, a kind of masturbation.
So what remains? Close friends, familiar places, family ties –
All so unique, it seems a crime to them to generalize
And say the love is more than love of him or her or it.
Apart from that there's nothing but the odd strange passing fit,
Times when one does seem to feel a love for everything:
Stoppages on the train returning home from work can bring
The mood – one sits, cheek resting on the cooling window-glass,
And idly looks around: the roofs, the scrubby trackside grass;
The clouds; the pale commuters as they read or muse or sleep;
And all so frail: but that love's of a kind to make me weep.

                    *   *   *

'ALL RIGHT' – the phrase I use when third-forms drive me up the
    pole,
And I resort to threats and punishments to gain control.
The trouble is I'm no damn good at ruling kids by fear:
I shut them up, but every smirking face conveys a jeer.

Nevertheless, ALL RIGHT, THAT'S IT, this time I'm really
  SERIOUS:
If love fails, I'll go back to spite, however deleterious
It'll be to what remains of my conventional reputation;
And this time, I assure you, there will be no hesitation,
No faltering or backsliding, no attempts to eat my words:
This time I mean to *bury* you all beneath my stinking turds,
Or let you bury yourselves; and don't expect to find it funny –
For if my stream has failed to reach its land of milk and honey,
I'll let it turn to shit again, make all our turds renew it.
It flows through drab South London, so let's all contribute to it:
Figures abound today, but I have read no estimation
Of how much piss and shit is passed by London's population –
Probably enough to drown us all if none of it were drained.
Think of the size of stream if all the *verbal* shit we rained
Were added to the flow, having achieved its rightful form;
And if we gave *ourselves*, oh what a stinking, squelching storm
Would rage perpetually, and what an all-engulfing flood!
Church-spires, tower-blocks, Parliament would sink beneath the
  mud.
For are we not just, in a sense, turds of the social maw?
We're born, and it digests us till we're 'grown-up' and 'mature';
Then throws us out as piss and shit to fertilize the earth
That grows the food that feeds the flesh that in its turn gives birth
To yet more social fodder; and a school *par excellence*
Shows how the social body's huge gut-processes advance.
The sweet young first-year kids are what the hideous monster eats:
Five years it spends digesting, then it thankfully excretes
What's left of them into the running sewer called the world.
My metaphor is stronger, yes, the more that it's unfurled.
What are the lives of all of us if not a nourishment
For the monster called Society, excreted when we're spent?
It eats, chews and digests us till it plops us in a hole:
The only freedom given us is to make the monster roll
And howl with stomach-ache, indeed we're so damn good at that,
It seems we'll be too much for him one day and AAH, OWW,
  SPLAT –
His stomach will explode from ulcers, poison and excess.
But no more of that *idée fixe*, I don't want to digress –

Back to the school; and first, the staff. Am I the only one
Who in our cramped foul masters' cloakroom gets some sordid fun
From watching all the ways we each compose ourselves to pee?
Some are embarrassed; others act as if they're taking tea,
And urinals were a splendid place for talking shop at break.
Some finish delicately, others with a mighty shake;
Our champion eccentric likes to stand with elbows spread
Upon the window-sill – he needs to rest his wooden head
Perhaps, it must be heavy – and discuss the news or weather.
Thank God we aren't obliged to sit and clear our bowels together,
Although I sometimes feel staff-meetings are precisely that:
Would we pass more rubbish if we didn't talk but shat?
Each teacher sits the way he would if he were defecating:
Some smoke, some do the crossword, others sit there meditating,
Each comment falls as heavy as do faeces in the pan.
The constipated colleagues keep us there as long as they can.
Sometimes someone jolts us with a fit of diarrhoea...

Seven Poems

The Bird

Dark is the vault that entombs the tomb
For a granite lid has sealed the doom
Of the paradise-bird, whose every plume
Was a fire to light its clammy gloom.
Oh until the last chink in the tomb
Was sealed, the vault was a dazzling room
For a single fiery feather or plume
Was enough to make its darkness bloom.
Shall the bird escape? Is the tomb a womb
For her bright re-birth? Or is it her doom
The fire of her feathers to self-consume
Till all without and within is gloom?

The Tree

'The tree is high and I am small,'
Says the boy to the oak, 'but I shall haul
Planks and nails to the top and install
The highest, grandest tree-house of all.'
'You do not know', says the oak, 'how you maul
My flesh with your nails. Wind blow! Boy crawl
Too far from the trunk and be too small
To reach that branch and Fall, Fall!
Let your father run at your terrified call.'
The roof of the rabbit-hutch breaks his fall.
Prone, he weeps for his high green hall,
His half-built grandest tree-house of all.

The Saint

The grip of her hands is warm with sin;
Her holiest smile is an impish grin.
Once she was proud of her hands' soft skin
And she washed and scrubbed to clear them of sin.
Right hand said, 'Wash again, there is sin
Still clinging to my delicate flawless skin.'
Left hand said, 'If I let you win
No man nor woman shall be her kin –
She must stick her arms in the rubbish-bin!
In the battle of the hands neither should win.'
The grip of her hands is kind with sin;
Her holiest smile is an impish grin.

The Healer

The sick, the maimed, the deaf, the blind,
The mad, the vile, the paralysed lined
The roads and at his touch would find
That they were cured. The healthy pined,
Because to those who are not blind
But cannot see, who are unconfined
But crippled, whole in body and mind
But hopeless, he says, 'I cannot bind
Invisible wounds; my touch is behind
All healing, but is not designed
To work a cure as undefined
And slow and cruel as you must find.'

The End

Scientist, dream of men who passed
On into space to flee the blast
Of sun destroying earth at last –
Earth will die but man will last.
Pietist, sing of souls who passed
To God from men whose faith held fast –
Man will die but God will last.
Satirist, laugh at God that he passed
Such power to creatures so ill-cast
And made his own iconoclast –
God will die and dust will last.
God will die and dust will last.

The Lake

We had to learn. We had to break
Asunder, tear our hearts to make
Wounds that could heal. O kind heart-ache,
O nightmares, blest if at last they wake
To this reconcilement! Look at the lake:
Our smiles join sun, join wind to rake
Its face into joy. We *do* partake,
Sometimes, of power that can sometimes shake
Life into beauty. The waters may quake
Coldly again; the spell will break;
But let us remember, for hope's sake,
Today our smiles walked on the lake.

The Child

Daughter of mine, your shining eyes
See no danger, no louring skies
Through the glass walls our lives comprise.
The walls are mirrors to you: back flies
Trust, light, until some cruel surprise,
Some meanness starts to undisguise
The fragile walls. But who is wise?
One who sees through? Or one whose eyes,
Like yours, can see light that defies
Transparency, who on darkening skies
Can superimpose constant sunrise?
Do you tell truth, my love, or lies?